W9-BZU-640

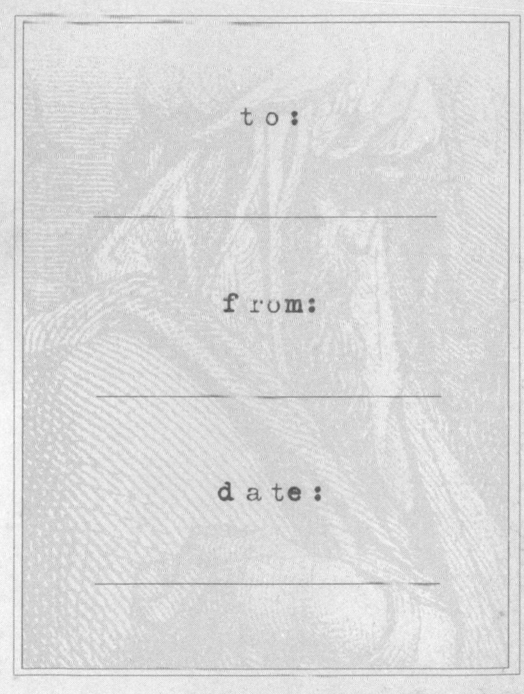

to:

from:

date:

JeSus FReaks:

A Journal

ALBURY
PUBLISHING

Tulsa, Oklahoma

Jesus Freaks: A Journal
ISBN 1-57778-209-7

Albury
Publishing

Published by Albury Publishing
P. O. Box 470406 / Tulsa, Oklahoma 74147-0406

Introduction

Dear Fellow Jesus Freak,

As passionate SEEkers of God, we all need an outlet sometimes. We've found journaling to be a great source for that outlet. We hope *Jesus Freaks: A Journal* will become a similar outlet for you.

There is so much inside of us that lONgs to be spoken, but not always with voice. You alone know all the things your heart yearns for—all the desires, big and small, that God has given you. Only you know the fears and doubts that plague your heart. To whom do you tell them? Sometimes you may feel like your problems are about to crush you. Tell God. Write them to Him in this journal. Your smallest cares may get lost in the rush of life. Don't let them. God wants to meet your needs, no matter how small they might seem.

In your journal, you can write down all your hopes, dreams, and burdens—every crazy thought that crosses your mind. You will be able to look back through your past journals and see where God has made a big move in your life, or fulfilled a simple desire. Each time we look back and see God's goodness to us—the "landmarks" of our lives—we REMember God's FAIThfulneSs. Every time God did something big for the Israelites, He told them to leave a mound

of stones to remind them and future generations of His faithfulness. (See, for example, Joshua 4:2-9.) We think of our journal as our personal landmark, our record of God's faithfulness and goodness to us.

Think of King David. He was called a "MAn after God's own heart." (1 Samuel 13:14). We love to read his "journals" in the Psalms. Look at how he wrote: he praised, shouted, cried, lamented, rejoiced, sang, declared, and poetically adored the Lover of his soul. He wrote his frustrations and anger out. He even asked God: "Where are You? I need You." (See Psalm 22:1-2.) When you write on these pages, make it real—as David did. Write of your passions, your joys, and especially your trials. Pour out your heart without reserve. Don't be afraid to question God here. Whatever you're feeling, this is the place to express it.

This is *Your* journal, so write in *YOUR* words and in *YOur* way. Some days you might write five words; some days the dam will break and you'll write ten pages. Just WRite. Make it a prayer, if that best suits your style. Be honest. Be bold. Don't be afraid. That's one thing we've learned from our fellow Jesus Freaks who've gone before us: hold nothing

back. Most of them were journalers. That's how we have their stories. If you will be open and honest with yourself, compromise and apology can't sneak in when you proclaim the Truth to others. Be solid. Be steadfast. And lastly, remember, Jesus Freak, your story must be told too.

■ dAte: / / ■ tiMe: ■ plAce:

WE shall not end our lives in the FIRE, but make a change for a better life.

JULIUS PALMER

Burned at the stake in England, 1556

■ dAte: / / ■ tiMe: ■ plAce:

"Love your enemies AND pray for those wHO persecute you."

JESUS

(Matthew 5:44 NIV)

■ dAte: / / ■ tiMe: ■ plAce:

This is THE END. For me, the beginning of LIFE.

DIETRICH BONHOEFFER

Hanged in Germany, 1945

■ dAte: / / ■ tiMe: ■ plAce:

"Father, forgive them, for they DO NOT KNOW what they do."

JESUS

(Luke 23:34 NKJV)

■ dAte: / / ■ tiMe: ■ plAce:

For to me, **living** is for Christ, and DYing is **even** BETTER.

PAUL THE APOSTLE

Beheaded in Rome, AD 65

(Philippians 1:21)

■ dAte: / / ■ tiMe: ■ plAce:

REMEMBER
the Lord's
people
who are
in JAIL
and be
concerned
for them.
DON'T
forget
those
who are
suffering,
but
IMAGINE
that YOU
are there
with them.

Hebrews
13:3 CEV

■ dAte: / / ■ tiMe: ■ plAce:

■ THOUGHT Starter:

Jesus said to "COUnt the cost." (See Luke 14:28-33.)

What does that mean for me?

COunt the COSt

■ dAte: / / ■ tiMe: ■ plAce:

■ dAte: / / ■ tiMe: ■ plAce:

I was in the CENtral highlands in Vietnam when someone remarked about HOW the Christians suffer there.

ONE Vietnamese Christian remarked, "Suffering is not the WORSt thing that can happen to us. Disobedience to God is the worst thing."

TOM WHITE

Director of The Voice of the Martyrs

Imprisoned in CUBA for 17 months for distributing Christian literature, 1979-80

a JouRNAl

■ dAte: / / ■ tiMe: ■ plAce:

"Brothers will give their OWN brothers to be killed, AND fATHERS will give their OWN children to be killed. Children will fight against their OWN parents AND HAVE them put to DEATH. All people will hate you because YOU foll o w ME, but those people who keep their FAITH until the end will be saved."

JESUS

(Matthew 10:21–22 NCV)

■ dAte: / / ■ tiMe: ■ plAce:

A CHRISTIAN prisoner in CuBA was asked to sign a statement containing charges against fellow Christians that would LEAD to their ARREST.

He said, "The chain keeps me from signing tHIS." The Communist OFFICER protested, "But YOU are not in chains!"

"I AM," said the CHRISTIAN. "I am bound by the chain of witnesses WHO throughout the CENTURIES gave their lives for JesusChrist. I am a link in this chain. I will not break it."

a JouRNAl

■ dAte: / / ■ tiMe: ■ plAce:

We CONTINUE to shout out praise even when we're HEMMED in with troubles, because we know how troubles can DEVELOP passionate patience in us, and how that patience in turn forges the tempered STEEL of VIRTUe, keeping us alert for whatever God will do next. In alert expectancy such as this, we're NEver left feeling shortchanged. Quite the contrary—we can't round up enough containers TO HOLD everything GOD generously pours into our lives through the Holy Spirit!

PAUL THE APOSTLE

Martyred in Rome, AD 65

(Romans 5:3–5 THE MESSAGE)

■ dAte: / / ■ tiMe: ■ plAce:

I live in a land ruled by THE FALSE teaching of Islam. MY people are blinded, and I was chosen by God to be His voice.

I count all that I have suffered nothing compared to the endless JOY of knowing JESUS, the WAY, the TRUTH, and the LIFE.

ZAHID

PAKISTAN

■ dAte: / / ■ tiMe: ■ plAce:

So WE always HAVE courage. We know that while we live in this body, we are away from the LORD. We live by what we BELIEVE, not by what we can see.... We really want to be away from this body and be at HOME with the Lord. Our only goal is to please GOD whether we live here or there.

PAUL THE APOSTLE

Martyred in Rome

AD 65

(2 Corinthians 5:6–9 NCV)

■ dAte: / / ■ tiMe: ■ plAce:

You NEVER KNOW HOW much you really BELIEVE anything until its TRUTH or falsehood becomes a MATter of LIFE and death to YOU.

C.S. LEWIS

■ dAte: / / ■ tiMe: ■ plAce:

"There will even come a time when anyone who KILLS you will think he's doing GOD a FAVOR. They will do these THINGS because they never really understood the Father. I'VE told you these things so that when the TIME comes and they start in on you, you'll be well-warned and READY for them."

JESUS

(John 16:2-4 THE MESSAGE)

■ dAte: / / ■ tiMe: ■ plAce:

The bandit told the missionary, "I'm going to KILL you. Aren't you afraid?"

Jack Vinson REPLIED simply, "Kill me, if YOU wish. I will go straight to GOD."

KIANGSU PROVINCE, MAINLAND CHINA, 1931

a JouRNAl

■ dAte: / / ■ tiMe: ■ plAce:

"WHOever declares openly—speaking out freely—AND confesses that he is MY worshipper AND acknowledges ME before men, the SON OF MAN also will declare and confess and acknowledge him before the angels of God."

JESUS

(Luke 12:8 AMP)

■ dAte: / / ■ tiMe: ■ plAce:

■ THOUGHT Starter:

This is a LETTER to a person who has challenged my FAITH.

LEtter to a FRIenD

■ dAte: / / ■ tiMe: ■ plAce:

■ dAte: / / ■ tiMe: ■ plAce:

A minister I had heard OF IN Romania had been horribly beaten and was thrown back into the CELL with the OTHER prisoners. HE was half-dead, with blood streaming from his face and BODY. As some of THE prisoners washed him, others cursed the Communists.

Groaning, the minister said, "Please, don't curse them! Keep silent! I wish to pray for them."

RICHARD WURMBRAND

Imprisoned for a total of 14 years, Romania, 1940s-60s

a JouRNAl

■ dAte: / / ■ tiMe: ■ plAce:

Through thick and thin, keep your HEARTS at attention, in adoration before Christ, your Master. Be ready to speak up and TELL anyone who asks why you're living the Way you are.

PETER THE APOSTLE

Martyred in Rome, AD 65

(1 Peter 3:14-15 THE MESSAGE)

■ dAte: / / ■ tiMe: ■ plAce:

SOME Christians haven't even attempted to think about whether or not they would DIE for Jesus because they haven't really been living for HIM.

DC TALK

a JouRNAl

■ dAte: / / ■ tiMe: ■ plAce:

JeSUS said that when we are mocked and persecuted because we are HIS followers we can be happy about it: "Be very glad! FOR A great reward AWaits you in HEAVEN."

JESUS

(Matthew 5:12)

■ dAte: / / ■ tiMe: ■ plAce:

It seems God is limited by our PRAYER LIFE– that He can do nothing for humanity unless someone ASKS Him.

JOHN WESLEY

Founder of the Methodist Movement

■ dAte: / / ■ tiMe: ■ plAce:

When a BELIEVING person **prays,** great things **happen.**

JAMES, THE JUST

Thrown from the temple wall, AD 63

(James 5:16 NCV)

■ dAte: / / ■ tiMe: ■ plAce:

GOD, accept all my sufferings, my tiredness, MY humiliations, my tears, my nostalgia, my being hungry, my SUFFERING of cold, all the bitterness accumulated in my soul. . . . Dear Lord, have pity on those who persecute and torture us day and night. Grant them, too, the DIVine GRACE of knowing the sweetness and happiness of YOUR love.

WOMAN PRISONER IN SIBERIA

VORKUTA, U.S.S.R., CIRCA 1960

a JouRNAl

■ dAte: / / ■ tiMe: ■ plAce:

"You're familiar with the old written law, 'LOVE YOUR FRIEND,' and its unwritten companion, 'Hate your enemy.' I'm challenging that. I'm telling you to LOVE your enemies. Let them bring out the best in you, not the worst. When someone gives you a hard time, respond with the energies of PRAYER, for then you are working out of your true selves, your GOD-CREATED selves. This is what God does. He gives his BEST to everyone."

JESUS

(Matthew 5:43-45 THE MESSAGE)

■ dAte: / / ■ tiMe: ■ plAce:

He is NO FOOL who gives what he cannot KEEP to gain what he cannot lose.

JIM ELLIOT

Speared by headhunters in Ecuador while serving there as a missionary, 1956

a JouRNAl

■ dAte: / / ■ tiMe: ■ plAce:

"Don't be BLUFFED into silence or insincerity BY THE threats of religious bullies. TRUE, THEY CAN KILL you, but then what can they do? There's nothing they can do to your SOUL, your core being. SAVE your fear for God, who holds your entire LIFE—BODY and SOUL—in his hands."

JESUS

(Luke 12:4,5 THE MESSAGE)

■ dAte: / / ■ tiMe: ■ plAce:

■ THOUGHT Starter:

How is it THAT people who don't even have a Bible, who've never even read one before, can HAVE AS MUCH faith as— or MORE faith than—I do?

COunt the COSt

■ dAte: / / ■ tiMe: ■ plAce:

■ dAte: / / ■ tiMe: ■ plAce:

Without fear we SANG in prisons 30 feet beneath the earth.

We were TERRIBLY hungry, beaten, and tortured.

The Communists were good at torturing us.

We would say to each other,

"The Communists beat us very well—let us do our work well. Let us sing well."

RICHARD WURMBRAND

IMPRISONED FOR A TOTAL OF 14 YEARS, ROMANIA, 1940s-60s

a JouRNAl

■ dAte: / / ■ tiMe: ■ plAce:

Let us run with endurance the race that God has set before us. We do this by keeping our eyes on Jesus, on whom our faith depends from start to finish. HE was willing to die a shameful death on the cross because of the joy he knew would be his afterward. NOW HE is seated in the place of highest honor beside God's throne in heaven. THINK about all he endured when sinful people did such terrible things to him, so that you don't become weary and give up.

Hebrews 12:1-3

■ dAte: / / ■ tiMe: ■ plAce:

Death is MUCH sweeter to me with the testimony OF truth than life with the least DENIAL.

GELEAZIUM

Martyred in St. Angelo, Italy, Middle Ages

a JouRNAl

■ dAte: / / ■ tiMe: ■ plAce:

DEAR friends, never avenge yourselves. Leave that to God. For it is written, "I will take vengeance; I will repay those who deserve it," says the LORD. Don't let evil get the best of you, but conquer EVIL by doing GOOD.

PAUL THE APOSTLE

Martyred in Rome, AD 65

(Romans 12:19,21)

■ dAte: / / ■ tiMe: ■ plAce:

Humanly speaking, we know that no one likes to SUFFER physically. But I know that if the Lord leads me into it, HE will give me the STRENGTH to survive it.

Pastor Li De Xian

Mainland China, 1990s

■ dAte: / / ■ tiMe: ■ plAce:

If God is with us, no one can defeat us. Can anything separate us from the LOVE Christ has for us? Can troubles or PROBLEMS or sufferings or hunger or nakedness or danger or violent DEATH? ...in all these things we have FULL victory through God who showed his love for us.

PAUL THE APOSTLE

Martyred in Rome, AD 65

(Romans 8:31,35, 37 NCV)

■ dAte: / / ■ tiMe: ■ plAce:

Do your worst, I am a Christian. CHRIST is my help and supporter, and thus armed I will never serve your gods NOR DO I fear your authority or that of your master, THE Emperor. Commence your torments as soon as YOU please, and make use of every means that YOUR malignity can invent, and YOU shall find in the end that I am not to be shaken from my resolution.

ADRONICUS

ROMAN EMPIRE, AD 303

a JouRNAl

■ dAte: / / ■ tiMe: ■ plAce:

DON'T forget about those in prison. Suffer with them as though you were there yourself. Share the SORROW of those being mistreated, as though YOU feel their pain in your own BODIES.

Hebrews 13:3

■ dAte: / / ■ tiMe: ■ plAce:

Let us **KEEP** our eyes steadily upon the GOAL.... For when we hear the shout from the skies, all else will fade into utter nothingness. For the Lord shall descend from heaven with a SHOUT. Even so, come, Lord Jesus.

ROBERT JAFFRAY

Parc-Parc Prison, New Guinea, 1945

a JouRNAl

■ dAte: / / ■ tiMe: ■ plAce:

WE'RE NOT keeping this quiet, not on your life. Just LIKE THE psalmist who wrote, "I believed it, so I said it," we say what we BELIEVE. And what we believe is that THE ONE who raised up the Master Jesus will just as certainly raise us up with you, alive. EVERY detail works TO YOUR advantage and to God's glory; more and more grace, more and more people, more and more PRAISE!

PAUL THE APOSTLE

Martyred in Rome, AD 65

(2 Corinthians 4:13–15 THE MESSAGE)

■ dAte: / / ■ tiMe: ■ plAce:

■ THOUGHT Starter:

There are "Creator's MARKS" in each of us—Unique characteristics God has chosen to define us. When people LOOK at me, what "Creator's MARKS" do they see?

DIvine bluePRInt

■ dAte: / / ■ tiMe: ■ plAce:

■ dAte: / / ■ tiMe: ■ plAce:

Angels are transparent. If an angel STANDS before you with a man behind him, the presence of the angel does not keep you from seeing the man. ON THE contrary: Looking at a MAN through an angel makes him more beautiful. I see my torturers through an ANGEL. In that way, even they become lovable.

IVAN "VANYA" MOISEYEV

MARTYRED IN THE U.S.S.R., 1972

■ dAte: / / ■ tiMe: ■ plAce:

WE ARE confident of all this because of our GREAT trust in God through CHRIST. It is not that we think we can do anything of lasting value by ourselves. Our only POWER AND SUCCESS come from God. He is the ONE who has enabled us to represent his new covenant.

PAUL THE APOSTLE

Martyred in Rome, AD 65

(2 Corinthians 3:4–6)

■ dAte: / / ■ tiMe: ■ plAce:

Suffering saints are LIVING SEED.

CHARLES SPURGEON

19TH CENTURY THEOLOGIAN

a JouRNAl

■ dAte: / / ■ tiMe: ■ plAce:

"Unless a grain of wheat is buried in the ground, DEAD to the world, it is never any more than a grain of wheat. But if it is buried, it sprouts and reproduces itself many times over. In the same way, anyone who holds on to life just as it is destroys THAT LIFE. But if you let it go, reckless in YOUR love, you'll have it forever, real and ETERNAL. If any of you want to serve ME, then follow me."

JESUS

(John 12:23–26 THE MESSAGE)

■ dAte: / / ■ tiMe: ■ plAce:

Now I suffer what I suffer; but then ANOTHER will be in me who will suffer FOR ME, because I too will be suffering for Him.

FELICITAS

Martyred in Carthage, North Africa, AD 202

■ dAte: / / ■ tiMe: ■ plAce:

Whether it's right in GOD'S eyes to listen to you rather than to God, YOU decide. As for us, there's no QUESTION—we can't keep quiet about what we've seen and heard.

(Acts 4:19-20 The Message)

■ dAte: / / ■ tiMe: ■ plAce:

I AM so thankful for the power of PRAYER. I received strength from God and was never ill—no flu, no skin disease, no illness at all. And I had lots of opportunities to share the Gospel with my fellow inmates.

ORSON VILA

IMPRISONED IN CUBA, 1995

■ dAte: / / ■ tiMe: ■ plAce:

Through your faithful PRAYERS and the generous RESPONSE of the Spirit of Jesus Christ, everything HE wants to do in and through me will be done. I can hardly wait to CONTINUE on my course.

PAUL THE APOSTLE

Martyred in Rome, AD 65

(Philippians 1:19-20 THE MESSAGE)

■ dAte: / / ■ tiMe: ■ plAce:

However IT GOES with me, I labor that you may have the Gospel preached among YOU. Though it cost my life, I think it well bestowed.

JOHN PEARY

Martyred in Wales, 1593

a JouRNAl

■ dAte: / / ■ tiMe: ■ plAce:

Act like people WITH GOOD sense and not like fools. These are evil times, so make EVERY minute count.... Find out what the LORD wants you to do.

PAUL THE APOSTLE

Martyred in Rome, AD 65

(Ephesians 5:15-17 CEV)

■ dAte: / / ■ tiMe: ■ plAce:

■ THOUGHT Starter:

What is my passion today? What is the LORD speaking to my heart?

HEart of paSSIon

■ dAte: / / ■ tiMe: ■ plAce:

■ dAte: / / ■ tiMe: ■ plAce:

A Communist officer told a Christian he was beating, "I AM almighty, as you suppose your God to be. I can kill you." The CHRISTIAN answered, "The power is ALL on my side. I can love you while you torture me to death."

■ dAte: / / ■ tiMe: ■ plAce:

What do Jesus Freaks do when betrayed by others close to them? They show them GOD'S LOVE.

Love [God's love in us]... takes no account of the evil done to it—pays no attention to a SUFFERED WRONG.... LOVE bears up under anything and everything that comes, is ever ready to believe the best of every person, its hopes are fadeless under all circumstances and it endures everything [without weakening].

PAUL THE APOSTLE

Martyred in Rome, AD 65

(1 Corinthians 13:5,7 AMP)

■ dAte: / / ■ tiMe: ■ plAce:

A Jesus Freak never faces his problems alone. God's Holy Spirit is ALWAYS there to give him COMFORT, STRENGTH, and HOPE.

a JouRNAl

■ dAte: / / ■ tiMe: ■ plAce:

LOOK at my servant, whom I strengthen. He is my chosen one, and I am pleased with him. I have put my SPIRIT upon him.

Isaiah 42:1

■ dAte: / / ■ tiMe: ■ plAce:

Atheists—those who DON'T BELIEVE in God or life after death—are amazed when Christians are ready to sacrifice their lives rather than DENY a God no one can see.

They don't understand the deep work of the Holy Spirit and how He makes both the Father's love and heaven an undeniable REALITY in the heart OF A believer.

■ dAte: / / ■ tiMe: ■ plAce:

For his Holy Spirit SPEAKS to us deep in our hearts and TELLS US that we are GOD'S children. And since we ARE HIS children, we will share his treasures—FOR everything God gives to his Son, Christ, is ours, too. But if we are to share his GLORY, we must also share his SUFFERING. Yet what we suffer now is nothing compared to the glory he will give us later.

PAUL THE APOSTLE

Beheaded in Rome, AD 65

(Romans 8:16-18)

■ dAte: / / ■ tiMe: ■ plAce:

The church has an unconditional obligation to the victims of any ordering of society. There are THINGS for which an uncompromising stand is worthwhile.

DIETRICH BONHOEFFER

Hanged in Germany for resisting the Nazis, 1945

■ dAte: / / ■ tiMe: ■ plAce:

I KNOW the Lord is always with me. I will not be shaken, for HE is RIGHT beside me. No wonder my heart is filled with joy, and my mouth SHOUTS his praises! You will show me the way of life, granting me the joy of your presence and the pleasures OF living with you forever.

Psalm 16:8–9,11

■ dAte: / / ■ tiMe: ■ plAce:

Throughout history, Jesus Freaks have sung during their final moments on earth. To the astonishment of their tormentors, they JOYFULLY raised their VOICES in praise to God.

a JouRNAl

■ dAte: / / ■ tiMe: ■ plAce:

For our present troubles are quite small and WON'T LAST very long. Yet they produce for us an IMMEASURABLY great glory that will last FOREVER! So we don't look at the troubles WE CAN SEE right now; rather, we look forward to what we have not yet seen. For the TROUBLES we see will soon be over, but the joys to come will last forever.

PAUL THE APOSTLE

Written after having been imprisoned, stoned and left for dead, shipwrecked, and tortured numerous times by those who opposed him

(2 Corinthians 4:17–18)

■ dAte: / / ■ tiMe: ■ plAce:

■ THOUGHT Starter:

My HEART loves to sing songs of praise to my Maker.

Which song was I singing THIS morning when I woke up, and what does it mean to me?

sIng a sONg

■ dAte: / / ■ tiMe: ■ plAce:

■ dAte: / / ■ tiMe: ■ plAce:

My Lord was pleased to DIE for my sins; why should I not be glad to give up my poor life out of love TO HIM?

GIROLAMO SAVANAROLA

Martyred, Florence, Italy, 1498

■ dAte: / / ■ tiMe: ■ plAce:

YOU intended to harm me, but God intended it for good to accomplish what is now being DONE, THE saving of many LIVES.

JOSEPH

Sold into slavery and later imprisoned, circa 1689 BC

(Genesis 50:20 NIV)

dAte: / / tiMe: plAce:

WORDS pronounced by martyrs before the authorities are not human words, the simple expression of a HUMAN conviction, but words pronounced by the HOLY SPIRIT through the confessors of faith.

Thomas Aquinas

■ dAte: / / ■ tiMe: ■ plAce:

Everything happening to me in this JAIL only serves to make Christ more accurately known, regardless of whether I LIVE or die. They didn't shut me UP; they gave me a pulpit! Alive, I'm Christ's messenger; dead, I'm his bounty. Life VERSUS even more life! I can't lose.

PAUL THE APOSTLE

Martyred in Rome, AD 65

(Philippians 1:20–21 THE MESSAGE)

■ dAte: / / ■ tiMe: ■ plAce:

You can kill us, but you cannot do us any real harm.

JUSTIN MARTYR

Martyred in Rome, AD 165

a JouRNAl

■ dAte: / / ■ tiMe: ■ plAce:

They defeated him (Satan) through the blood of the LAMB and the bold word of their witness. They weren't in love with themselves; they were willing to die FOR Christ.

JOHN THE APOSTLE

Tortured and exiled, Roman Empire, AD 97

(Revelation 12:11 THE MESSAGE)

■ dAte: / / ■ tiMe: ■ plAce:

My dear **Jesus,** MY **Savior,** is so **deeply written** in my **heart,** that **I feel** confident, that **if** my **HEART** were to be **cut open** AND **chopped** to **pieces,** the **name** of **JESUS** would be **found** written on **every** piece.

IGNATIUS

A student under John

Devoured by wild animals in Rome, AD 111

a JouRNAl

■ dAte: / / ■ tiMe: ■ plAce:

"Do not FEAR any of those things which you are about to suffer. Indeed, the devil IS ABOUT TO throw some of you into prison, that you may be tested, and YOU will have tribulation ten days. Be faithful until death, and I will give you the crown of life."

JESUS

(Revelation 2:10 NKJV)

■ dAte: / / ■ tiMe: ■ plAce:

I BLESS God for my imprisonment, for I then began to relish the LIFE and sweetness of God's Holy Word.

NICHOLAS CAREN

Martyred in England, 1539

■ dAte: / / ■ tiMe: ■ plAce:

God deliberately chose things the WORLD considers foolish in order to shame those who think they are WISE.... so that no one can ever boast in the presence of God. As the Scriptures say, "The person who wishes to boast should boast only of what the LORD has done."

Paul the Apostle

Beheaded in Rome, AD 65

(1 Corinthians 1:27,29,31)

■ dAte: / / ■ tiMe: ■ plAce:

■ THOUGHT Starter:

IF IT were illegal to be a Christian, WHAT evidence would there be to convict me?

LIve the FAIth

■ dAte: / / ■ tiMe: ■ plAce:

■ dAte: / / ■ tiMe: ■ plAce:

Even THE BEST of Christians are troubled by the QUESTION, "Why does an almighty God send, or at least allow, suffering?" When YOU are nagged by thoughts like this, SAY TO yourself, "I AM still in elementary school. When I GRADUATE from the university of Christian life, I will understand His ways better and doubts will cease."

RICHARD WURMBRAND

Imprisoned for a total of 14 years, Romania, 1940s-60s

■ dAte: / / ■ tiMe: ■ plAce:

The ETERNAL God is your refuge, and underneath are the everlasting arms.

Deuteronomy 33:27 NIV

■ dAte: / / ■ tiMe: ■ plAce:

Unless I AM convinced by Scripture and plain reason—I do not accept the authority of the popes and councils, for they have contradicted each other—my conscience is captive to the Word of God. I cannot and I will not recant anything FOR TO GO against conscience is neither right nor safe. GOD help me. Amen.

MARTIN LUTHER, 1483-1546

Father of the Reformation

Tried for heresy, 1521

a JouRNAl

■ dAte: / / ■ tiMe: ■ plAce:

"My grace is enough; it's all you need. MY strength COMES into its own in your weakness." It was a case of Christ's strength moving in ON MY weakness. Now... I just let CHRIST take over! And so the weaker I get, the stronger I become.

PAUL THE APOSTLE

Martyred in Rome, AD 65

(2 Corinthians 12:9-10 THE MESSAGE)

■ dAte: / / ■ tiMe: ■ plAce:

Two Chinese Christians were led to TORTURE and DEATH. One quoted Jesus' WORDS, "It is finished," in a whisper. His brother answered, "No, that's not what Jesus said when He suffered. He said, 'It is accomplished.'"

a JouRNAl

■ dAte: / / ■ tiMe: ■ plAce:

I'm ABOUT TO DIE, my life an offering on God's altar. This is the only race worth running. I've run hard right to the finish, believed all the way. ALL that's left now is the shouting—God's applause! Depend on it, he's an honest JUDGE. He'll do right not only by ME, BUT BY everyone eager for HIS coming.

PAUL THE APOSTLE

Martyred in Rome, AD 65

(2 Timothy 4:7–8 THE MESSAGE)

■ dAte: / / ■ tiMe: ■ plAce:

I tell you this so you won't be ashamed by my death. If you love me, you will rejoice that GOD has called me to this honor, which is GREATER THAN any earthly honor I could ever attain.

Who wouldn't be happy to DIE for this cause? I trust in my LORD GOD, who put His mind, will, and affection in my heart, and choose to lose all my worldly substance, and my life, too, rather than deny His known truth. HE WILL comfort me, aid me, and strengthen me forever, even to the yielding of my spirit and soul into His hands.

Bishop Nicholas Ridley

Burned at the stake, Oxford, England, 1555

■ dAte: / / ■ tiMe: ■ plAce:

If PEOPLE persecute you because you are a Christian, don't curse them; pray that God will bless them. When others are happy, be happy with them. If they are SAD, share THEIR sorrow. Don't let evil get the best of you, but conquer evil by DOING good.

PAUL THE APOSTLE

Martyred in Rome, AD 65

(Romans 12:14-15,21)

■ dAte: / / ■ tiMe: ■ plAce:

While in JAIL, we sang. Once the director of the prison entered our cell, furious. "I was told that you sing subversive songs here.

Let me hear one," he commanded. We sang these moving WORDS: "O sacred Head, now wounded, with grief and shame bowed down. . . ." He listened to the end, then turned and left without saying a word. Later he became a brother in the faith.

RICHARD WURMBRAND

Imprisoned for a total of 14 years, Romania, 1940s-60s

■ dAte: / / ■ tiMe: ■ plAce:

A GENTLE response defuses anger.

Proverbs 15:1

THE MESSAGE

■ dAte: / / ■ tiMe: ■ plAce:

■ THOUGHT Starter:

This is a prayer for the PERSON who gives me the hardest time about being a Jesus FREAk.

LOve your ENEmy

dAte: / / tiMe: plAce:

■ dAte: / / ■ tiMe: ■ plAce:

Do not be ASHAMED by my DEATH. I think it is the greatest honor of my life and thank God for calling me TO GIVE MY life for His sake and in His CAUSE. He gave the same honor to the holy prophets, His dearly BELOVED apostles, and His blessed, CHOSEN martyrs. I have no doubt that I am dying for God's cause and the cause of truth.

PERPETUA

CARTHAGE, NORTH AFRICA, AD 202

a JouRNAl

■ dAte: / / ■ tiMe: ■ plAce:

Such LOVE has no fear because perfect love expels all fear. If we are AFRAID, it is for fear of JUDGment, and this shows that HIS love has not been perfected in us. We love each other as a result of his LOVING us first.

JOHN THE APOSTLE

Exiled to Patmos, AD 95

(1 John 4:18-19)

■ dAte: / / ■ tiMe: ■ plAce:

Jesus is EVERY-thing.

MOTHER TERESA

Gave her life to the poor of India

DIED IN 1997

■ dAte: / / ■ tiMe: ■ plAce:

Because I PREACH this Good News, I am suffering and have been chained like a criminal. But the word of GOD cannot be chained. I am willing to endure anything if it will bring salvation and eternal glory in Christ Jesus to those God has chosen.

PAUL THE APOSTLE

Martyred in Rome, AD 64

(2 Timothy 2:9-10)

■ dAte: / / ■ tiMe: ■ plAce:

Lord GOD, these men take away my life full of misery, but You will give me LIFE everlasting.

Maurice Blanc

Martyred in Merindol, 1547

a JouRNAl

■ dAte: / / ■ tiMe: ■ plAce:

"These things I have spoken to you, that in ME YOU may have peace. In the world you have tribulation, but take courage; I have overcome the world."

JESUS

(John 16:33 NASB)

dAte: / / tiMe: plAce:

The Orthodox BISHOP Andrew of Ufa was sentenced to death. The story is told that before the execution, he asked to be allowed to pray.

As he knelt, he simply was no more. The henchmen were in a panic, knowing they would lose their LIVES if he disappeared. After an hour he reappeared on his knees, in PRAYER, surrounded BY A luminous CLOUD. The sentence was carried out, but one of the henchmen was converted and told the story.

■ dAte: / / ■ tiMe: ■ plAce:

In ALL their affliction He was afflicted.

Isaiah 63:9 NASB

dAte: / / tiMe: plAce:

"Don't be upset when they haul you before the CIVIL authorities. Without knowing it, they've done you—and me—a favor, given you a platform FOR preaching the kingdom NEWS! And don't worry about what you'll say or how you'll say it. The right WORDS will be there; the Spirit of your FATHER will supply the words."

JESUS

(Matthew 10:17-20 THE MESSAGE)

a JouRNAl

■ dAte: / / ■ tiMe: ■ plAce:

"Count yourselves blessed every time people PUT YOU down or throw you out or SPEAK LIES about you to discredit me. What it means is that the TRUTH is too close for comfort and they are uncomfortable. YOU can be glad when that happens—give a cheer, even!—for though they don't like it, I DO! And all HEAVEN applauds."

JESUS

(Matthew 5:11–12 THE MESSAGE)

■ dAte: / / ■ tiMe: ■ plAce:

■ THOUGHT Starter:

Which character in the BIBLE do I identify with most?

Why?

fOLLoWer of GOd

■ dAte: / / ■ tiMe: ■ plAce:

■ dAte: / / ■ tiMe: ■ plAce:

Dear FRIENDS, don't be surprised at the fiery trials you are going through, as if something strange were happening TO YOU. Instead, be very glad—because these trials will make YOU partners with Christ in his suffering, and afterward YOU will have the wonderful joy of sharing his glory when it is displayed to all the world.

PETER THE APOSTLE

Martyred in Rome, AD 65

(1 Peter 4:12-13)

a JouRNAl

■ dAte: / / ■ tiMe: ■ plAce:

My LIFE is worth nothing unless I use it for doing the work assigned me by THE Lord Jesus—the work of telling others the GOOD NEWS about God's wonderful kindness and love.

PAUL THE APOSTLE

Martyred in Rome, AD 65

(Acts 20:24)

■ dAte: / / ■ tiMe: ■ plAce:

For we DO NOT want you to be unaware, brethren, of our affliction which came to us in ASIA, that we were burdened excessively, beyond our strength, so that we despaired even of life; indeed, we had the sentence of death within ourselves in order that we should not TRUST IN ourselves, but in GOD who raises the dead; who delivered us from so great a peril of death, and will deliver us . . . you also joining in helping us through your PRAYERS, that thanks may be given by many persons on our behalf for the FAVOR bestowed upon us through the prayers of many.

PAUL THE APOSTLE

Martyred in Rome, AD 65

(2 Corinthians 1:8–11 NASB)

■ dAte: / / ■ tiMe: ■ plAce:

Let all who take refuge in you be glad; let them ever sing for joy. Spread your protection over them, that those who love your name may rejoice in you. For surely, O LORD, you bless the righteous; YOU surround them with YOUR favor as with a shield.

Psalm 5:11-12

NIV

■ dAte: / / ■ tiMe: ■ plAce:

"If any of YOU want to be my followers, you must forget about yourself. You must take up your cross and follow me. If you want to save your life, you will destroy it. But if you GIVE UP your life for me and for the good news, you will save it. . . . Don't be ashamed of me and my message among these unfaithful and sinful PEOPLE! If you are, the Son of Man WILL BE ashamed of you when he comes in the glory of his Father with the holy angels."

JESUS

(Mark 8:34-35,38 CEV)

a JouRNAl

dAte: / / tiMe: plAce:

Open your MOUTH for the speechless, in the cause of all who are appointed to die. Open your mouth, judge righteously, and plead the cause of the POOR and needy.

Proverbs 31:8-9 NKJV

■ dAte: / / ■ tiMe: ■ plAce:

Finally, let the mighty strength of the LORD make you strong. Put on all the armor that GOD GIVES, so you can defend yourself against the devil's tricks. We are not fighting against humans. We are fighting against forces and authorities and against rulers of darkness and powers in the spiritual world. So put on all the ARMOR that God gives. Then when that evil day comes, you will be able to defend YOURSELF. And when the battle is over, you will still be standing FIRM.

PAUL THE APOSTLE

Martyred in Rome, AD 65

(Ephesians 6:10-13 CEV)

■ dAte: / / ■ tiMe: ■ plAce:

Raising HIS EYES in prayer, [Jesus] said... "I spelled out your character in detail to the men and women you gave me. They were yours in the first place; then YOU gave them to me.... Everything mine is yours, and yours mine, and my life is on display in them. For I'm no longer going to be visible in the world: THEY'LL continue in the world while I return to you. Holy Father, guard them as they pursue this life that you conferred as a gift through me, so they can be one heart and mind as we are one heart and mind."

Jesus

(John 17: 1,6,10,11 The Message)

■ dAte: / / ■ tiMe: ■ plAce:

I've got my eye on the goal, where GOD is BECKONING us onward—to Jesus. I'M OFF AND running, and I'm not turning back. So let's keep focused on that goal, those of us who want everything GOD has for us. If any of you have something else in mind, something less than total commitment, God will clear your blurred vision—you'll see it YET!

PAUL THE APOSTLE

Martyred in Rome, AD 65

(Philippians 3:13-15 THE MESSAGE)

■ dAte: / / ■ tiMe: ■ plAce:

Though YOU have not seen him, you love him; and even though you do not see him now, you believe in HIM AND are filled with an inexpressible AND glorious JOY, for YOU ARE receiving the goal of your faith, the salvation of your souls.

PETER THE APOSTLE

Martyred in Rome, AD 65

(1 Peter 1:8–9 NIV)

■ dAte: / / ■ tiMe: ■ plAce:

■ THOUGHT Starter:

Jesus Freaks understand the temporary nature of this LIFE because they have a vision of eternity.

Is eternity in my spiritual vision?

VIsion of ETErnity

■ dAte: / / ■ tiMe: ■ plAce:

■ dAte: / / ■ tiMe: ■ plAce:

Sufferings **gladly** borne for others CONVERT MORE **people** than **sermons.**

THERESE OF LISIEUX

a JouRNAl

■ dAte: / / ■ tiMe: ■ plAce:

We work HARD and suffer much in order that people WILL believe the truth, for our hope is in the living GOD, who is the Savior of all people.

PAUL THE APOSTLE

Martyred in Rome, AD 65

(1 Timothy 4:10)

■ dAte: / / ■ tiMe: ■ plAce:

"YOU are My servant, I have chosen you and have not CAST you away: fear not, for I am WITH you; be not dismayed, for I am your GOD. I will strengthen you, yes, I WILL help you, I will uphold you with My righteous right hand."

Isaiah 41:9-10 NKJV

a JouRNAl

■ dAte: / / ■ tiMe: ■ plAce:

I never knew all there was in the Bible until I spent those years in JAIL. I was constantly finding new treasures.

JOHN BUNYAN

Imprisoned for a total of 12 years, England, 1660s–70s

■ dAte: / / ■ tiMe: ■ plAce:

"People need more than BREAD for their life; they must feed on every word of God."

JESUS

(Matthew 4:4)

dAte: / / tiMe: plAce:

"A SERVANT is not greater than the MASTER. Since they persecuted me, naturally they will persecute YOU. And if they had listened to ME, THEY would listen to you! The people of the world will hate you because you belong to me, for they don't know God who sent me."

Jesus

(John 15:20-21)

■ dAte: / / ■ tiMe: ■ plAce:

NO TEST or TEMPTATION that comes your way is beyond the course of what others have had to face. ALL you need to remember is that God will never let YOU DOWN; he'll never let you be punished past your limit; HE'LL always be there to help you come through it.

PAUL THE APOSTLE

Beheaded in Rome, AD 65

(1 Corinthians 10:13 THE MESSAGE)

■ dAte: / / ■ tiMe: ■ plAce:

VERY rarely will anyone DIE for a righteous man, though for a good man someone might possibly DARE TO DIE. But God demonstrates his own love for us in this: While we were still sinners, Christ DIED for us.

PAUL THE APOSTLE

Martyred in Rome, AD 65

(Romans 5:7–8 NIV)

■ dAte: / / ■ tiMe: ■ plAce:

WHATEVER we do, it is because Christ's LOVE controls us.... those who receive his new life WILL no longer live to please themselves. Instead, they will LIVE to please Christ, who died and was raised for them.

PAUL THE APOSTLE

Martyred in Rome, AD 65

(2 Corinthians 5:14–15)

■ dAte: / / ■ tiMe: ■ plAce:

SIN LOSES ITS power over us when we lay our lives down for Christ—because our eyes are on Jesus.

DC TALK

dAte: / / tiMe: plAce:

THOUGHT Starter:

Because we can't always see GOD'S HAND on our lives, we sometimes misunderstand His actions. This is a situation in my LIFE where that is the case.

the HAnd of GOd

■ dAte: / / ■ tiMe: ■ plAce:

dAte: / / tiMe: plAce:

Since **Jesus** went though everything YOU'RE going through and more, learn to think **like him.** Think of YOUR sufferings as a weaning from that old sinful habit of always expecting to get your own way.

Then you'll be able to **live out** your days free to pursue what God wants instead of BEING tyrannized by what you want.

PETER THE APOSTLE

CRUCIFIED UPSIDE-DOWN IN ROME, AD 65

(1 Peter 4:1–2 THE MESSAGE)

■ dAte: / / ■ tiMe: ■ plAce:

"We've GIVEN UP everything to follow you," [Peter] said. And Jesus replied, "I assure you that everyone who has given up house or brothers or sisters or mother or FATHER or children or property, for my sake and for the GOOD NEWS, will receive now in return, a HUNDRED times over, houses, brothers, sisters, mothers, children, and property—with persecutions. And in the world to come they will have eternal life."

JESUS

(Mark 10:28-31)

■ dAte: / / ■ tiMe: ■ plAce:

Many FEAR suffering; in the PAST, I too feared. But the presence of the LORD in jail has given me so many happy experiences that I would not have changed them for years of easy living in freedom.

BORIS (PSEUDONYM)

Imprisoned in the U.S.S.R.,

1970's

a JouRNAl

■ dAte: / / ■ tiMe: ■ plAce:

We are CHRIST'S ambassadors, and GOD is using US TO speak to you. We urge you, as though Christ himself were here pleading with you, "Be reconciled to God!"

PAUL THE APOSTLE

Martyred in Rome, AD 65

(2 Corinthians 5:20)

■ dAte: / / ■ tiMe: ■ plAce:

Nothing between us AND God, our faces shining with the brightness of his face. And so we ARE transfigured much like THE Messiah, our lives gradually becoming brighter and more beautiful as GOD enters our lives and we become like him.

PAUL THE APOSTLE

Martyred in Rome, AD 65

(2 Corinthians 3:18 THE MESSAGE)

■ dAte: / / ■ tiMe: ■ plAce:

For to me, living is for CHRIST, and dying is even better. Yet if I live, that means fruitful service for Christ. I really don't know which is better. I'm torn between two desires: Sometimes I want to live, AND sometimes I long to go and be with CHRIST. That would be far better for me, but it is better for you that I live. I am convinced of this, so I will continue with you so that you will grow and experience the joy of YOUR faith.

PAUL THE APOSTLE

Written while in prison awaiting execution; he was released some time later

(Philippians 1:21–25)

▪ dAte: / / ▪ tiMe: ▪ plAce:

The Father is a merciful God, who always gives us comfort.... We share in the terrible sufferings of Christ, but also in the wonderful comfort he gives.

PAUL THE APOSTLE

MARTYRED IN ROME, AD 65

(2 Corinthians 1:3,5 CEV)

a JouRNAl

■ dAte: / / ■ tiMe: ■ plAce:

PEOPLE who live in this way make it plain that they are looking for their TRUE HOME.... They were after a far better country... heaven country.... You can SEE why God is so proud OF them, and has a City waiting for them.

Hebrews 11:14,16
THE MESSAGE

■ dAte: / / ■ tiMe: ■ plAce:

For our light affliction, which is but for a MOMENT, is working for us a far more exceeding and eternal weight of glory, while we do not look at the things which are SEEN, BUT at the things which are not seen. For the things which are seen are temporary, but the things which are NOT SEEN are eternal.

2 Corinthians 4:17–18 NKJV

■ dAte: / / ■ tiMe: ■ plAce:

For God has Said, "I will never FAIL you. I will never forsake you." That is why we can say with confidence, "The Lord is my helper, so I will not be afraid. What can mere mortals do to me?"

Hebrews 13:5-6

■ dAte: / / ■ tiMe: ■ plAce:

■ THOUGHT Starter:

These are the areas of my LIFE in which God is training me right now. This is how I'm doing and how I have grown.

ArEas of GROwth

■ dAte: / / ■ tiMe: ■ plAce:

■ dAte: / / ■ tiMe: ■ plAce:

We're not giving up. How could we! Even though on the outside it often looks like things are falling apart on us, on the inside, where God is making new life, not a day goes by without his unfolding grace. These hard times are small potatoes compared to the coming GOOD TIMES, the lavish celebration prepared for us. There's far more here than meets the EYE. The things we see now are here today, gone tomorrow. But the things we can't see now will last forever.

PAUL THE APOSTLE

Martyred in Rome, AD 65

(2 Corinthians 4:16-18 THE MESSAGE)

■ dAte: / / ■ tiMe: ■ plAce:

In Mainland CHINA, A SWORD was put to the chest of a Christian.

He was asked, "Are you a Christian?"

He answered, "Yes."

He would have been killed if an officer had not said, "Free him; he is an IDIOT."

Someone asked him later, "How could you confess Christ with such courage?"

He replied, "I had read the story of Peter's denial of Jesus, and I did not wish to weep bitterly."

■ dAte: / / ■ tiMe: ■ plAce:

Here is a TRUE message: "If we died with Christ, we will live with him. If we don't give up, we will rule with HIM. If we deny that we know him, he will deny that he knows us. If we are NOT faithful, he will still be faithful. CHRIST cannot deny who he is."

PAUL THE APOSTLE

Martyred in Rome, AD 65

(2 Timothy 2:11-13 CEV)

a JouRNAl

■ dAte: / / ■ tiMe: ■ plAce:

Don't ever FORGET those early days when you first learned about Christ. Remember how you remained faithful even though it meant terrible SUFFERING. Sometimes you were exposed to public ridicule and were beaten, and sometimes you helped others who were suffering the same things. YOU suffered along with those who were thrown into JAIL. When all you owned was taken from you, you accepted it with joy. You knew you had better things waiting for you in eternity.

Hebrews 10:32-34

■ dAte: / / ■ tiMe: ■ plAce:

Where GOD'S love is, there is no FEAR, because God's perfect love DRIVES out fear.

JOHN THE APOSTLE

Tortured and exiled, Roman Empire, AD 95

(1 John 4:18 NCV)

a JouRNAl

■ dAte: / / ■ tiMe: ■ plAce:

I prayed to the LORD, and he answered me, freeing me from ALL my FEARS. Those who look to him for HELP WILL BE radiant with joy; no shadow of shame will darken their faces.

Psalm 34:4-5

■ dAte: / / ■ tiMe: ■ plAce:

God doesn't take **BACK** the gifts he has **GIVEN** or **forget** about the **people** he has **chosen.**

PAUL THE APOSTLE

Beheaded in Rome, AD 65

(Romans 10:29 CEV)

a JouRNAl

■ dAte: / / ■ tiMe: ■ plAce:

Stand united, SINGULAR in vision, contending for people's trust in the Message, the good news, not flinching or dodging in the slightest before the opposition. Your courage and unity will show them what they're up against: defeat for them, victory for you—and both because of GOD.

Paul the Apostle

Martyred in Rome, AD 65

(Philippians 1:27-28 The Message)

Endnotes

Cuban Prisoner Quotation (p. 18)

Wurmbrand, *In the Face of Surrender,* 138.

Siberian Prisoner Prayer (p. 34)

Ibid., p. 23.

Geleazium Quotation (p. 42)

Lockyer, p. 145.

Robert Jaffray Quotation (p. 48)

Ibid., p. 154.

Felicitas Quotation (p. 56)

Chenu, p. 70.

John Peary Quotation (p. 60)

Lockyer, p. 148.

Girolamo Savanarola (p. 76)

Lockyer, pp. 150-51.

Prisoner Quotation (p. 88)

Wurmbrand, *In the Face of Surrender,* pp. 21-22.

Two Chinese Prisoners Quotation (p. 92)

Ibid., p. 224.

Richard Wurmbrand Quotation (p. 96)

Wurmbrand, *In the Face of Surrender,* p. 21.

Chinese Christian's Quotation (p. 149)

Ibid., p. 185.

Where Do I Find out More about Martyrs?

Where we got our information...

Chenu, Bruno, et al. *The Book of Christian Martyrs.* Translated by John Bowden. New York: The Crossroads Publishing Company, 1990.

Christian History: Dietrich Bonhoeffer. Vol. X, no. 4 (1991).

Christian History: John Bunyan. Vol. V, no. 3 (1986).

Grant, Myrna. *Vanya.* Lake Mary, FL: Creation House, 1974.

Hefley, James and Marti. *By Their Blood: Christian Martyrs of the Twentieth Century.* Second edition. Grand Rapids, MI: Baker Books, 1996.

Faith Under Fire, 30-minute videocasesette, produced and directed by Stephen Yake, The Voice of the Martyrs, 1998.

The Faithful, 15-minute videocassette, produced and directed by Stephen Yake, Steve Green Ministries and The Voice of the Martyrs, 1998.

Foxe, John. *Foxe's Book of Martyrs.* Prepared by W. Grinton Berry. Grand Rapids, MI: Baker Book House, 1998.

Johnstone, Patrick. *Operation World: A Day-by-Day Guide to Praying for the World.* Grand Rapids, MI: Zondervan Publishing House, 1993.

Lockyer, Herbert. *Last Words of Saints and Sinners.* Grand Rapids, MI: Kregel Publications, 1969.

Tortured for Christ, 30-minute videocassette, Department of Mission to Europe's Millions, Inc., 1967.

The Voice of the Martyrs monthly newsletters (formerly known as *Jesus to the Communist World*). Issues ranging from 1968 to 1999.

Van Braght, Thieleman J. *Martyrs Mirror.* Translated by Joseph F. Sohm. Scottsdale, PA: Herald Press, 1660.

White, Tom. *God's Missiles Over Cuba.* Bartlesville, OK: Living Sacrifice Book Company, 1981.

In God's Underground. Edited by Charles Foley. Bartlesville, OK: Living Sacrifice Book Company, 1968.

In the Face of Surrender: Over 200 Challenging and Inspiring Stories of Overcomers. New Brunswick, NJ: Bridge Logos Publishers, 1998.

Tortured for Christ. Bartlesville, OK: Living Sacrifice Book Company, 1967.

Other Suggested Titles...

Anderson, Ken, *Bold as a Lamb: Pastor Samuel Lamb and the Underground Church of China.* Grand Rapids, MI: Zondervan Publishing House, 1991.

Between Two Tigers. Compiled by Tom White. Bartlesville, OK: Living Sacrifice Book Company, 1996.

Edwards, Brian, *God's Outlaw: The Story of William Tyndale and the English Bible.* Darlington, England: Evangelical Press, 1976.

Foxe, John. *The New Foxe's Book of Martyrs.* Rewritten and updated by Harold J. Chadwick. New Brunswick, NJ: Bridge-Logos Publishers, 1997.

Hanks, Geoffrey. *70 Great Christians: Changing the World.* Fearn, Scotland, Great Britain: Christian Focus Publications Ltd., 1992.

Sheikh, Bliquis. *I Dared to Call Him Father.* With Richard H. Schneider. Grand Rapids, MI: Chosen Books, 1978.

Whalin, W. Terry, et al. *One Bright Shining Path: Faith in the Midst of Terrorism.* Wheaton, IL: Crossway Books, 1993.

Wurmbrand, Richard. *From Suffering to Triumph!* Grand Rapids, MI: Kregel Publications, 1991.

Wurmbrand, Sabina. *The Pastor's Wife.* Bartlesville, OK: Living Sacrifice Book Company, 1970.

About dc Talk

Toby McKeehan **Michael Tait** **Kevin Max**

Since releasing their album *Jesus Freak*, dc Talk has emerged as a leader in the pursuit of melding rock 'n' roll with provocative questions of faith.

Although various rock predecessors have examined spiritual issues—U2, Van Morrison, and Bob Dylan immediately come to mind—dc Talk has taken the notion to new lengths, both in commercial terms and depth of artistic exploration. Numerous Dove Awards, three Grammy Awards, two platinum albums, one gold album, and two gold-certified long-form videos attest to the group's ability to bridge the gap between religious and secular audiences.

Toby, Michael, and Kevin first met in the mid-80s while attending college in Virginia. After relocating to Nashville, dc Talk released a series of increasingly ambitious—and successful—albums, beginning with their self-titled 1989 debut. Following albums included: their gold-certified 1990 sophomore album, *Nu Thang;* the platinum-certified 1992 opus *Free at Last;* 1995's *Jesus Freak*—a platinum-plus watershed that afforded the group more mainstream success than ever before—and 1998's *Supernatural,* which reflected the maturity and sophistication of their latest stage of development and growth.

In 2000, while on a hiatus from recording and traveling, the group released *intermission,* a greatest hits recording which also included two brand-new songs. For the year 2001, the group will have collectively released four new CDs: each member will release a solo album, and their CD titled Solo includes two songs from each of the guys' upcoming solo projects.

Their first book, *Jesus Freaks,* has made a tremendous impact, challenging people to stand up for their Savior. Now, with forthcoming *Jesus Freaks* books, dc Talk continues to encourage each of us to go further in the quest to know and to make known our Lord and Savior, Jesus Christ, whatever the cost.

JESUS FREAKS

LIVE LIKE A JESUS FREAK

JOURNAL

PROMISES FOR A JESUS FREAK

Look for THese other GREAT BOOKS in the Jesus Freaks series.

Available everywhere books are sold.

Additional copies of this book and other book titles from **Albury Publishing** are available from your local bookstore.

Albury Publishing
P. O. Box 470406 • Tulsa, Oklahoma 74147-0406

For a complete list of our titles, visit us at our Web site:

www.alburypublishing.com

For international and Canadian orders, please contact:

Access Sales International
2448 East 81st Street • Suite 4900 • Tulsa, Oklahoma 74137
Phone 918-523-5590 Fax 918-496-2822